THE CARDINAL'S KITCHEN

Not a novel, not a history book, simply a little guide to good eating

by
Paola Greco

Dedicated to the memory of my mother

Foreword

Enjoying a good meal requires good company as much as the dishes themselves. In Paola Greco's 'little guide to good eating', the dishes enjoyed by popes and cardinals in times past are combined with her own Italian recipes. These recipes stimulate the imagination when it comes to show how different ingredients might be joined together, along with a savouring of the seasons and the occasions for dining. It has been a joy for me to share many of these dishes with friends and colleagues alike.

I would like to congratulate Paola for her care in putting these pages together. She has cooked many of these dishes for me personally. May she continue to cook and bring pleasure to others for many years to come.

+Cormac Card. Murphy-O'Connor

+Cormac Card. Murphy-O'Connor
Archbishop Emeritus of Westminster

HE Cardinal Cormac Murphy-O'Connor was appointed the tenth Archbishop of Westminster on 15th February 2000 and was previously Bishop of Arundel and Brighton. He was created a Cardinal by Pope John Paul II on 21st February 2001. After 9 years in Westminster Diocese he finally retired in 2009 and is now entitled, Archbishop Emeritus of Westminster.

Contents

Contents

Contents

Acknowledgements

My sincere thanks go to the Cardinal for allowing the writing of this book and for generously giving me such good introduction!

Also my heartfelt appreciation goes to my family especially to my husband Luigi and to my son Matt who have been subjected to an endless torture during the production of this book! They have been my guinea pigs and have been very patient, I am grateful to them! My thanks also to my son-in-law James who has taken many of the pictures in this book.

And thanks to my daughter Nicky and to my friend Virginia who have graciously "volunteered" to proof read my work thus giving up some of their week ends' precious time!

The history references and anecdotes have been taken from various websites and reference books. Wikipedia, bonappetit and foodtimeline have been my main sources.

Introduction

The idea of producing this "cookbook" came when I was asked to cook for the Cardinal and his assistant Monsignor for a couple of days a week. How could I refuse to provide nourishment for such esteemed mouths?

It is worth remembering that throughout the centuries, members of the Church from Popes, Cardinals, Bishops and Monsignors to the Parish Priests and Monks, all have been famously known for their love of the good table and for exotic food and tastes! I was therefore hoping to be ready for the challenge when I agreed to become the Cardinal's chef!

It has to be said that the Cardinal and the Monsignor had modest needs and were also happy with a simple bowl of pasta or soup followed by cheese or a dessert; on occasions though, especially when they had guests, they liked something a little more sophisticated.

Only on rare occasions, when they were eating on their own and the Cardinal had just come back from a game of golf (which he was not allowed to practice much due to the many commitments his position imposed on him), I would prepare something a little more elaborate and in larger quantity.

Mazur/catholicnews.org.uk

Brief historical notes

St Peter *(Public domain)*

Throughout the centuries famous clergymen became associated with food. We can begin with St Peter, the first Pope, although his eating habits might be a little difficult to corroborate. He was a fisherman and certainly fond of fish! The legend goes that one day he was looking at one of his catches, the thorny little John Dory, also known as Peter's fish, and having pity for its ugly appearance, picked it up from his net with his thumb and forefinger thus giving him a pair of black spots which made it more appealing!

It is said that Pope Innocent III (1161-1216), who was one of the mediaeval Church's most powerful Popes, was very partial to wine with a passion for Verdicchio (white Italian wine grown primarily in the Marche region) which he used to drink from golden goblets.

Pope Innocent III
(Public domain)

From the food that people ate, from Roman times to mediaeval times, we have a better appreciation of how they lived as food is a significant component of the different cultures. Not many recipes were written down in what we know as recipe books as many people were not literate; recipes were passed down from generation to generation and it may well be that a particular dish we eat today is an "amendment" of a dish eaten by our progenitors. Some of the recipes given in this guide, are recipes that my grandmother used to prepare for us and no doubt the same recipes were passed down to her by her grandmother.

Rodrigo Borgia
(Public domain)

Many are the historic figures somehow connected with the Church who have left a mark in the culinary field. For instance, in 1615, when the Spanish princess Anne married King Louis XIII of France, she brought with her the recipe for chocolate as part of her offering and the first documented chocolate consumer in France was Cardinal Richelieu, who enjoyed it as a delicious treat but also to help the digestive system. Rodrigo Borgia, better known as Pope Alexander VI (1431-1503), and Cesare Borgia, Cardinal of Valencia (1475-1507), had their own particular taste in food and it seems that all their meals were prepared by Lucrezia Borgia and by her sister-in-law for fear of being poisoned! The Borgias were rumoured to be in possession of a special poison called La Cantarella, nicknamed the "liquid of succession", which was probably made with arsenic that was particularly lethal and used to kill their political rivals. And because it had no taste, it was almost impossible to detect. So, not a good sign to be invited to dine with the Borgias! Although this rumour has never been proven, it was believed in diplomatic circles that Cesare had his brother Juan murdered by poison.

Brief historical notes (continued)

Perhaps he was helped in this by his sister Lucrezia as they were very close. So not a good sign to be invited to dine with the Borgias! Lucrezia Borgia had a hollow ring which was said to contain the toxic mixture that was used to poison their rivals with. Lucrezia has become the typical example of an unscrupulous, shameless and dangerous woman and has been the subject of many works of literature and art. Regardless of their ruthlessness and ambition, the Borgias' way of dealing with rivals and politics gave Machiavelli the inspiration for his The Prince; and although Machiavelli opens his work with a dedication to Lorenzo de Medici (1449 – 1492) who was in practice the ruler of Florence and one of the most influential figures of the time, it was Cesare Borgia who captivated his imagination and he described him as an example of "criminal virtue". His work was controversial and was before long condemned by the Church.

Cesare Borgia
(Public domain)

Other Popes lived in fear of being poisoned. Pope Boniface VIII (1235-1303) was terrified of this. It was said that his tableware was made of gold and therefore, for fear of being robbed and killed, he employed a full-time food taster and had all sorts of talismans. He even had a magic knife which seemed to detect poison by touching the poisoned food!

Pope Boniface VIII
(Public domain)

All sorts of soups and broths; roasts and cheeses; salads with different sauces were served at the Renaissance table; a curious fact is that salt was not used much as in many countries the salt tax was so high that it made salt almost as dear and hard to obtain as some Indian spices and therefore used only by the very rich.

Many soups were served at the same time, they all had a rich taste and were made with expensive ingredients; they were considered to be extravagant and only eaten by the nobility. King Francis I of France (1494 – 1547) loved soups and so did the French, as they do today. They declare to be the creators of more than seventy soups!

It was already customary in the 15th century to eat salads with or after the roasted meats or fishes. They were dressed like we do today with oil, salt and other spices.

An interesting fact is that pasta was introduced to France by Charles VIII (1470 – 1498) after an expedition to conquer the Italian peninsula and all the pastas were from then on called Italian dishes as they originated from Italy.

My recipes

Mine is not meant to be a cookery book as I realise that I cannot compete with the experts! It is simply a collection of some very nice recipes that I have assembled through the years or have started to make recently and that I have prepared for the Cardinal in his kitchen.

The recipes contained in this little collection are some of my invention but also inspired by meals I had at friends' and relatives' houses. You will also recognise well known recipes which have been "adapted" to make them more interesting. They are given as an indication of what you could offer your guests on different occasions and in different seasons of the year. Most of these recipes are very easy to make with only some being a little difficult and laborious. Remember, cooking is an art and a real remedy for boredom and, although there is no magic formula for happiness, a good meal comes very close to real satisfaction. And the best way to enjoy a good meal is to start it when you are hungry. A French proverb says that a meal ought to begin with hunger!

Remember, do not eat in excess or else you may end up among those placed by Dante with the gluttons (from the Latin word *gluttire*, which means to gulp down) in his *Divine Comedy* (in the third circle and in the fourth level of his *Inferno*, gluttons were constantly being eaten by demons) and I believe a few representatives of the Florentine clergy were among them! Pope Martin IV, for example, (1281–1285) was certainly one of the Popes placed by Dante in Purgatory as he was one of the gluttonous Popes (at the time, for political reasons, he could not place him in hell). Dante talks about his strong interest in eels from the nearby Lake of Bolsena which were cooked in Vernaccia wine (one of Italy's finest white wines produced in the San Gimignano area, near Siena). His passion for good food led him to die of indigestion!

My recipes (continued)

Giovanni Della Casa, also known as Bishop Monsignor Della Casa or Dellacasa, Apostolic Nuncio in Venice, and author in 1558 of the manual of good manners or *Etiquette overo de costumes*, enjoyed fresh pasta, exclusive fowl dishes with truffle and fresh products, all eaten in moderation. In his book, he denounces every excess and embodies the cult of proportion, typical of the Renaissance.

I must not digress too much from the task in hand...and before you start reading my guide, please keep in mind that I am not a chef by profession.

The recipes in this collection alternate with anecdotes and stories I read about while thinking of dishes that I could prepare in the "Cardinal's kitchen" and while "exploring" various websites to get ideas.

I remember that to impress the honourable commensals (from the Latin *cum mensa*, meaning sharing a table), I spent a few days trying to think of unusual Italian regional recipes that would be appreciated as an introduction to my cooking and to prove my ability as a cook. I failed to take into consideration that both the Cardinal and the Monsignor were very familiar with Italian cooking having lived in Italy for quite some time and therefore very difficult to satisfy. The Cardinal jokingly used to give me a rating on a scale from 1 to 10 according to his satisfaction.

The Cardinal has a very good sense of humour. I remember that one evening, he had invited my two bosses, a Bishop and a Monsignor, to dine with him knowing perfectly well that I was working with them. He called me when they were having an aperitif before dinner and introduced me to them with these words: "meet the chef"! He certainly achieved the desired reaction as the Bishop and the Monsignor were quite surprised to see me there!

On a pleasant spring evening...
... my very first attempt as the Cardinal Chef!

So, for my first exploit in the Cardinal's kitchen, this is what I prepared on a pleasant spring evening: *Couscous salad, rocket & pear salad, involtini di tacchino (stuffed turkey fillets) and strawberries in red wine.*

Couscous salad
Ingredients and method

100g Couscous

200ml hot water made with 1 vegetable stock cube if you prefer

1 courgette

1 red pepper

1 yellow pepper

1 green pepper

1 aubergine

1 white onion (the sweet variety)

1 half/packet of dried apricots (tinly cut)

Ingredients for the dressing: salt, pepper, honey (acacia or very mild), extra-virgin olive oil, juice of half lemon, balsamic vinegar garlic and cloves. Leave the garlic and cloves to soak in the oil, lemon and vinegar for an hour or so.

Preheat the oven to 200°/gas 6. Dice all the vegetables in tiny pieces. Put them in an oven dish with two tbsp. extra-virgin olive oil and salt and bake for approx. 30 minutes or until brown, mixing occasionally. While the vegetables are baking tip the couscous into a large bowl and cover with hot water (or stock). Keep covered until the water has been soaked up. When the couscous is ready fork through the vegetables and the cut apricots. Remove the garlic and cloves from the dressing, pour into vegetable couscous and blend all ingredients nicely.

Rocket & pear salad
Ingredients and method

1 packet rocket salad

2 Rocha pears

1 tbsp. crushed walnuts

2 tbsp. extra-virgin olive oil, balsamic vinegar, salt pepper

Thinly slice the pears, add to rocket and walnuts. Dress with extra-virgin olive oil, balsamic vinegar, salt and pepper.

Involtini di tacchino (stuffed turkey fillets)
Ingredients and method

6 turkey fillets – same size (chicken can be used instead)

6 slices pancetta

6 (or more) gorgonzola cheese small pieces

cranberry sauce

¼ cup flour

salt

Preheat oven to 180°. Beat the fillets with a steak hammer so that they become fairly thin. Sprinkle them with flour on both sides and season with a little salt. On each fillet spread some gorgonzola cheese, cover with cranberry sauce, roll the fillets and place them on a strip or two of pancetta. Roll the pancetta around the fillets and close with a toothpick. Place the fillets in a single layer in an oiled oven dish and cook for 10/15 minutes. When serving, use the juice that has come out during cooking to cover the fillets.

Not many people may know that one of the first recipes for turkey was invented by the second Medici Pope's (Pius IV – 1499-1565)) chef, Bartolomeo Scappi, as shown in his 900-page work illustrating his abilities as a cook ("Opera dell'arte del cucinare"). In his book he gives more than 1,000 recipes of the Renaissance cuisine and describes various tools in precise details. He was the first to assert that Parmesan was the best cheese in the world!)

Given that he was in charge of the Vatican kitchen under seven Popes (1534 – 1576) he must have witnessed a few "extravagant events" during his life as the Popes' chef!

Strawberries in red wine
Ingredients and method

200g punnet strawberries

1 tsp cane sugar

1 glass (pinot or Lambrusco) red wine

Wash the strawberries quickly under running water (without removing the stalks), dry with kitchen towel and remove the stalks. Cut the strawberries in small pieces. Put them in a bowl; cover them with the sugar dissolved in the wine. Mix well and put them in the fridge for an hour or so.

Verdict

I think my first trial went quite well as the Cardinal gave me an eight! But I was striving to get a 10, so I kept on trying!

One summer evening...

Strawberries again....you must try the strawberry risotto I made on my next attempt: *Risotto con fragole (strawberry risotto) - scaloppine al Marsala, lime cheese cake*

Strawberry risotto
Ingredients and method

200g Italian Arborio rice.

300ml vegetable stock (1 cube)

200g strawberry
(Remember not to remove the stalks when washinh the strawberries)

50g fresh single cream

50g parmesan cheese

2 tbsp. extra-virgin olive oil

20g unsalted butter

Half onion, thinly sliced

1 garlic clove

Heat the oil in a large pan over a medium-low heat. Add the onion, garlic and butter and cook stirring often for a few minutes until the onion is soft. Add the rice and stir until it is well coated. Remove the garlic. Add a little white wine (optional) and cook until it has been absorbed. Add the stock a little at the time and cook gently; half way through, add the washed, cut strawberries (but leave two strawberries for decoration), always stirring to avoid sticking and continue adding stock until all the stock has been used and until the rice is cooked. Season with a little salt according to taste. If you think the rice is not ready, add a little more stock. Fold in a little cream and stir one last time. Remove from the heat (my grandma used to always finish her risotto by adding a knob of butter so that the rice is nice and creamy), add the Parmesan cheese and serve in two individual plates; place a strawberry on top of each portion for decoration.

King Henry VIII should be credited for inspiring the marriage of strawberries and cream. Cardinal Wolsey (1473-1530), the right hand of the King was famous for having large crowds to feed in his palace at Hampton Court; working in one of the largest kitchens during Tudor times must have been quite a nightmare as it is believed that King Henry VIII's court was made up of about 1,200 members; it must have been a blessing to "discover" a dessert that took very little time to prepare! It is most unlikely that Cardinal Wolsey himself came up with the idea of combining strawberries and cream but perhaps someone in Wolsey's kitchen had an inspired moment and discovered that blending strawberries and cream made a delicious dessert! And this would seem to be the most logical explanation as dairy products were considered by the "nobility" to be food for peasants. And certainly the unknown genius, probably a scullery boy/girl dreaming of becoming a famous chef, would never have imagined that his/her amalgamation of products would still be served all over the world and enjoyed by millions, in particular by the Wimbledon fans!

Scaloppine al Marsala
Ingredients and method

¼ cup flour

4 thinly cut boneless/skinless chicken breast

2 tbsp. extra-virgin olive oil

¼ cup marsala wine (Sherry can be used instead)

10g unsalted butter

Vegetable stock (½ cube)

Chopped parsley (optional)

Place the flour on a plate and coat the chicken on both sides. Heat the oil in a large non-stick pan over a medium-high heat. Place the chicken in the pan and cook for 2-4 minutes on each side; add the marsala and cook for another minute or so scraping any bits from the pan. Add the stock, salt and pepper (optional). Cover the pan and cook gently for 15 minutes.

In many parts of Italy in August, during the Feast of the Assumption, the statue of Our Lady is processed in the streets and there are many events to commemorate the occurrence. The celebration culminates with a banquet, and in Tuscany Scaloppine al Marsala is the appropriate dish for the occasion!

Lime cheese cake
Ingredients and method

Zest of 1 lime

Juice of 1 lime

1 tub mascarpone cheese (250g)

1 tub quark cheese (250g)

1 packet digestive biscuits (300g) - crumbled

100g butter

150g icing sugar

Melt the butter in a pan and mix with the biscuits so that they are all coated. Press them evenly in the pan and put in the fridge.

Mix the mascarpone and the quark together with the zest and the juice of the lime and the icing sugar until you have a thick creamy mixture. Remove the base from the fridge, pour the cream on top and level with a knife. Sprinkle some lime zest on the cake. Put in the fridge for a couple of hours before serving.

An autumn evening...

When the Cardinal had guests he would ask me to prepare something a little different and more elaborate. So, on my second effort, when he invited a Lord and Lady friends to dinner I thought of the following which went down quite well! *Crêpes salad - salmon en croute with sautée asparagus - castagnaccio (chestnut cake)*

Crêpes salad
Ingredients and method

100g flour

2 eggs

Milk 1 cup (or enough to have a smooth but not liquid batter), some use water as well but I prefer using milk only)

2/3 tbsp. melted butter

Salt, 3-4 basil leaves

3 salad tomatoes

30g Parmesan cheese

Mix the flour and the eggs and whisk together; add the milk slowly, the melted butter and the salt, blending all the ingredients until you obtain a smooth batter. Heat a non-stick pan (better still if you use a proper crêpes dish), grease the bottom of the pan and put a scoop of batter into it using roughly ½ cup for each crêpe. By tilting the pan you make sure that the batter is evenly distributed. Cook the crêpe for about 1 or 2 minutes until the bottom is golden brown, then turn it with the help of a spatula and cook briefly the other side. Once the batter is

all finished, leave the crêpes to cool down, cut them in thin slices (they should look like short tagliatelle) and put them in a large bowl. Cut the tomato in small chunks; grate a generous piece of Parmesan cheese (large side of the grater). Place the three ingredients together in the bowl so that the three colours stay separate (to form an Italian flag). Pour some extra-virgin olive oil and salt on the salad and take it to the table as it is before mixing the ingredients together with some basil leaves.

You may not know that Pope Gelasius I (V century) might have fortuitously come up with the crêpe in France. When, during a newly created holiday thousands of people came from afar on a pilgrimage to Rome, Pope Gelasius ordered his cooks to produce some simple pancakes to distribute among the hungry. When the pilgrims went back to their countries over the Alps, among the memories they also took back the crespelle which developed into the modern crêpe.

Salmon en croute with sautée asparagus
Ingredients and method

250g puff pastry (you can cheat here and buy it in supermarkets or you can make your own but it takes much longer!)

2 salmon fillets (organically grown or wild salmon), skinned

zest of 1 lemon, finely grated and 1 tbsp. of lemon juice

100g unsalted butter

1 tbsp. fresh parsley

1 clove garlic

1 egg, beaten

salt to taste

1 bunch of fresh asparagus

Start by seasoning the salmon fillets with salt. Mix the butter, lemon zest and juice with the parsley, garlic and a little salt in a food processor and blend until a paste is formed. Cut the pastry into two parts and on a floured surface roll each piece and give it a rectangular shape slightly larger than the salmon slice. Put the salmon fillets on one side of each rectangle. Distribute the paste equally on top of the two fillets and then brush the pastry edges with some egg (you can also use milk if you prefer), then fold the other side of the pastry over the salmon. Brush again with egg or milk and use a fork to seal the edges. Make some 2-3 incisions on the top. Preheat oven to 200° and bake for 20 minutes or until golden.

While the salmon is cooking, steam the asparagus (washed) in a covered pan for 5 minutes; heat some butter in a pan and cook the asparagus for a further 5 minutes adding some salt and turning occasionally. When the salmon is ready, serve on the same dish with the asparagus on one side and the salmon on the other.

Castagnaccio (chestnut cake)
Ingredients and method

750 ml water

500g chestnut flour

100g pine nuts

1 tbsp. fresh needles rosemary

80g raisins (optional)

salt to taste

6 tbsp. extra-virgin olive oil

zest of one orange

Preheat the oven to 200° half an hour before mixing the ingredients. Soak the raisins in warm water (if you are using them); sift the flour in a large bowl so it comes with no lumps; add a generous pinch of salt, pour a little of the water at a time into the chestnut flour and stir with a whisk until you have a smooth mixture. If you use raisins remove them from the water, dry them and mix them with the mixture together with the pine nuts (leaving some to put over the surface). Oil a shallow pan (40 cm diameter) making sure you cover the whole surface, pour the mixture in (about 1 inch in height) and finally sprinkle with the rosemary, the rest of the pine kernels and the orange zest. Bake for 30 minutes or until a golden crust has formed.

It is difficult to prove where the chestnut cake has its origin as many regions in the north have their own version; however, over time, the cake has become more associated with Tuscany. It is especially associated with the town of Siena. Chestnuts were eaten by poor people and were mainly used in rural areas. It is certain though that this cake was already known in '500 as a Father Augustine describes it in one of his literary works. A commentary written by Hortensius Orlando and published in Venice indicated that Tuscany was the heart of the chestnut. Starting from '800 the Tuscan chestnut was exported to the rest of Italy and the cake was enriched with raisins, pine nuts and rosemary.

Talking about chestnut....... Cesare Borgia (him again), Cardinal of Valencia, was the host of infamous banquets, the most famous being the Banquet of Chestnuts where he would ask his courtesans, at different levels of intoxication and in the company of women of dubious reputation, to pick up chestnuts, disseminated on the floor, on their hands and knees.

Enjoy anytime of the year...

Mozzarella, tomato, avocado and basil salad - Pear and taleggio cheese risotto - pear cooked in red wine

Mozzarella, tomato, avocado and basil salad
Ingredients and method

2 buffalo mozzarella

1 ripe avocado

200g cherry tomatoes

4 or 5 basil leaves for decoration

Salt, pepper, extra-virgin olive oil

Cut the buffalo mozzarella, the avocado and the tomatoes into thick slices and arrange nicely on a large dish separating the ingredients according to the colour. Season with salt, pepper, extra-virgin olive oil and decorate with basil leaves.

Pear and taleggio cheese risotto
Ingredients and method

200g Italian Arborio rice.

300ml vegetable stock (1 cube)

200g taleggio cheese

2 ripe pears (abate)

50g parmesan cheese

2 tbsp. extra-virgin olive oil

20g unsalted butter

Half onion, thinly sliced

1 garlic clove

The preparation of this risotto is initially very much like the strawberry risotto. Heat the oil in a large pan over a medium-low heat. Add the onion, garlic and butter and cook stirring often for a few minutes until the onion is soft. Add the rice and stir until it is well coated. Remove the garlic. Add a little white wine (optional) and cook until it has been absorbed. Add the stock a little at the time and cook gently; half way through, add the thinly cut pears and keep stirring; when the rice is almost cooked, add the taleggio cheese (remove the skin) cut into small pieces and stir until it has completely melted. Remove from the heat; add a little butter and the Parmesan cheese.

Pear cooked in red wine
Ingredients and method

2-3 abate pears, skinned, left whole with stalk, 50g sugar, 1 glass red wine, water, 2-3 cloves, a hint of cinnamon

Place the skinned, whole pears (do not remove the stalk) in a saucepan with the wine and water (1 glass), the sugar, cloves and cinnamon. Let the liquid come to a boil, cover and let cook over a gentle heat turning the pears occasionally. Remove from the heat when a thick sauce has formed and the pears are cooked but firm. Use a strainer to filter the sauce and cover the pears with it.

I was able to listen to the conversation at the Cardinal's table from my advantageous position through the kitchen opening into the dining room while preparing the food. It was always interesting. Not that I wanted to listen, but this was unavoidable! And sometimes they would include me in the conversation and I would speak through the opening. Some of the Cardinal's guests had connections with Italy, either through relatives living there or through personal knowledge and it was therefore very pleasant to speak about our common experiences; inevitably, the main subjects of discussion were art and food!

Some facts on northern Italy food

As you may know, Italy is made of 20 regions, each with its very own character and food specialities. I was born and grew up in Milan, in Lombardy where one of the main characteristic dishes is the famous "risotto" (the most famous being the "risotto allo zafferano" or saffron risotto) which you can easily enjoy in any Italian restaurant in the UK today but which is also very easy to make at home. Another speciality which has become very famous in this country thanks to the many programmes about food we enjoy on television, is Bresaola, a raw beef fillet which is cured in salt then air-dried for several months, also a speciality of Lombardy and sometimes served as an alternative to Parma ham. And the famous cheeses found in supermarkets all over the country like Robiola, Crescenza, Taleggio, Gorgonzola and Grana Padano, all come from Lombardy.

As a vegetarian I am not inclined to cook meat much. Nevertheless, as I respect other people's tastes and choices, the following were presented on my next attempt *Bresaola with rocket and Parmesan cheese - fillet of beef with rocket - cherry chocolate meringue pots*

Bresaola with rocket and Parmesan cheese
Ingredients and method

1 packet (100g bresaola), ½ packet wild rocket, Parmesan cheese (shavings)

Arrange the rocket salad on a wide dish, place the bresaola and the Parmesan cheese on top; season with a little salt, olive oil and lemon juice.

The French Cardinal Jacques de Vitry (13th Century) in his sermons used to describe the sellers of cooked meat as endangering people's health; I too think that meat should be eaten in moderation (if you must). Perhaps the reason for Cardinal de Vitry's dislike of meat was the fact that he was heavily involved in the Crusades and might have witnessed the suffering of many animals!

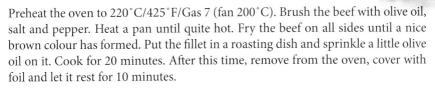

Fillet of beef with rocket
Ingredients and method

> 500g beef fillet, ½ packet rocket salad
>
> 2 tbsp. extra-virgin olive oil
>
> Salt
>
> pepper

Preheat the oven to 220°C/425°F/Gas 7 (fan 200°C). Brush the beef with olive oil, salt and pepper. Heat a pan until quite hot. Fry the beef on all sides until a nice brown colour has formed. Put the fillet in a roasting dish and sprinkle a little olive oil on it. Cook for 20 minutes. After this time, remove from the oven, cover with foil and let it rest for 10 minutes.

Spread the rocket salad on a serving dish and when the fillet has cooled, cut it in thick slices and place on the rocket.

Cherry chocolate meringue pots
Ingredients and method

This was taken from BBC good food (serves 4), it is delicious and very easy to make, ideal if you have little time to prepare a dessert.

> 300ml pot double cream
>
> 4 meringues nests, roughly broken
>
> 50g dark chocolate
>
> 8 tbsp. cherry compote

Whip the cream to soft peaks, then fold in the meringue pieces. Heat the chocolate in the microwave for 30-45 seconds or until melted, stirring halfway through. Spoon 2 tbsp. cherry compote into each of 4 glasses, then top with meringue mix. Drizzle melted chocolate on top of each glass and serve.

....and speaking of cherries, did you know that Pope Gregory 1st, also known as St Gregory the Great (540AD - 604AD), had a real passion for cherries? Once, during the month of April, he had a real craving for cherries and as it was a little too early in the season for that fruit, it seemed impossible that his servants could satisfy his wishes. But St Mark appeared in a cloud of fire to one of his gardeners and, having blessed a cherry tree, this bloomed with ripe cherries.

Flavours of Liguria

From Milan the family moved to Genoa, Liguria; I think this region offers one of the most surprisingly varied cuisine, with lots of fish dishes on the Riviera and meat, walnuts, pine kernels and chestnuts in the hinterland. The specialities of the Ligurian cuisine are made to traditional recipes with typical regional products. The Ligurian cuisine combines herbs, olive oil, which is mainly produced in the province of Imperia and other centres in the provinces of Savona and La Spezia, with pasta, meat and cheese to offer an incredible variety of delicate and tasty dishes. The pesto, the well-known basil based sauce comes from here and the delicious walnut sauce also originates from Liguria.

However, when planning to serve dishes containing nuts, it is always advisable to ask whether any of your guests has an allergy to them as not everyone is free to eat anything they wish. As I said, walnut sauce is delicious, but can be very filling so try to plan something light to follow.

I remember that time when the Cardinal had a South African Bishop friend dining at his house and as I was planning to offer the ravioli with the walnut sauce, I asked him the question about allergies. "Paola" - he said - "the only thing I am allergic to, is not eating"!

Pesto crostini and stuffed eggs
Ingredients and method

1 bunch basil leaves

½ clove garlic

2 tsp pine kernels

100g Parmesan cheese

1 tbsp. breadcrumbs

2 tbs. extra-virgin olive oil

4/6 slices ciabatta bread (or similar)

4 hard-boiled eggs

1 tsp capers

1 tsp pickled gherkins

3 tbsp. mayonnaise

Pesto should be made by using a mortar and pestle but a food processor can also be used to save time. Place the basil leaves (washed and thoroughly dried) in the food processor with the garlic, the pine kernels, the Parmesan cheese and the breadcrumbs, add some olive oil and salt to taste. Process until you obtain a smooth cream. Cut some thick slices from a ciabatta loaf and toast them until golden and then spread the pesto sauce on them. If the sauce is too thick, add some water.

Cut the eggs in half, remove the yolk from the hard boiled eggs making sure not to break the skin. Add the yolks to the mayonnaise and to the finely chopped gherkins and capers and make a smooth, creamy sauce, add some salt. Fill the empty egg whites halves with the sauce.

Pansoti in walnut sauce

(this recipe takes time to make but the end result is fantastic)

Ingredients and method

For the ravioli:

> 150g flour (type 00)
>
> 50g white wine
>
> 50g water
>
> Salt

For the filling:

> 200g spinach
>
> 100g ricotta cheese
>
> 1 egg
>
> 25g Parmesan cheese
>
> Salt – pepper
>
> Marjoram (½ tsp)
>
> 1 clove garlic
>
> 20g extra-virgin olive oil

For the sauce:

> 100g walnuts
>
> 20g pine nuts
>
> ½ tsp chopped garlic
>
> 20g Parmesan cheese
>
> 2g marjoram
>
> 20g bread crumbs
>
> 100g milk (room temperature)

Mix together the flour and the salt in a large bowl, add the white wine and the water. Mix all the ingredients working with your hands until you get consistent, smooth dough. Cover with cling film and put in refrigerator for at least 30 minutes. While the dough is in the fridge, prepare the filling. Sieve the ricotta in a closed-meshed sieve over a bowl, cover with film and place in the refrigerator (this will be used for the filling). Wash the spinach and dry well. Pour the olive oil and garlic into a frying pan then add the spinach. Let it cook for about 5 minutes, season with salt, pepper and marjoram. Remove the garlic. Place the spinach in a sieve to let it drain until all the water has gone. Finally chop the spinach with a knife and place again on a colander to make sure that all the water is gone. In a large bowl mix the egg, salt and pepper and whisk well. Take the ricotta cheese you had placed in the fridge and mix it in the bowl with the egg. Mix until smooth and creamy. Add the marjoram, grated Parmesan cheese and the spinach. Mix all the ingredients until you have a homogeneous mixture. Put aside. Prepare the walnut sauce by putting the breadcrumbs in half a glass of milk. Put the walnuts, pine nuts, Parmesan cheese, the garlic and the marjoram in a blender (you can use a mortar if you prefer), add the softened breadcrumbs and blend until you get a thick cream (add some milk and olive oil during blending). Keep aside.

Knead the dough that you had left in the fridge on a slightly floured board; using a rolling pin try to obtain a thin sheet; cut from it squares of 7-8 cm. Put a spoonful of the spinach filling in the centre of each square leaving 1 cm of border to close the pansoti. Brush the edges of the squares with water, milk or egg yolk and close the pansoti in the shape of a triangle; press lightly with your fingers to seal the pansoti and to prevent the filling from coming out during cooking. Repeat the process until all the dough has been used. Arrange the pansoti ready for cooking on a floured surface, cover them.

Bring water to the boil in a large pan, add salt. Pour the pansoti into the water one by one and cook for 4-5 minutes on a medium heat. When the pansoti rise to the surface remove them from the water and place them on a large dish. Add some of the cooking water to the walnut sauce, mix well and dress the pansoti with it.

P.S. The sauce can be used with pasta like penne or tagliatelle, less time consuming and you could buy the spinach and ricotta cheese ravioli available in most supermarkets! Pesto is also excellent with potato gnocchi.

Chocolate mousse
Ingredients and method

100g (very good quality) dark chocolate

50 ml milk

150ml double cream

Melt the chocolate in a bowl over a pan of simmering hot water. Boil the milk and whisk in the melted chocolate. Leave to cool. Whip the cream until soft then fold in the cooled chocolate. Spoon the chocolate mixture into small bowls and put in refrigerator. You can add a little sugar if needed as dark chocolate can be bitter.

It seems that chocolate mousse (French for foam) originated in France in the 18th century. Only the very best dark chocolate was used. There are many variations to this recipe with some using egg whites and butter and others adding sugar as dark chocolate can be very bitter.

Vegetarian friends

When planning your meal it is very important to remember your vegetarian friends, they will be very happy to see that you have made provision for them. The following are some appetizers and dishes which are both delicious and not very laborious to make and will keep not only your vegetarian, but also your non vegetarian guests satisfied. *Tomato bruschetta - courgette and leek quiche - stuffed mushroom and tomatoes - fruit salad in lemon juice*

Tomato bruschetta
Ingredients and method

200g sweet, ripe tomatoes

5/6 leaves basil

sea salt

pepper

extra-virgin olive oil

4/6 slices of bread (ciabatta cut in chunks of 1 cm)

Toast the bread (in a toaster or a griddle pan). Lightly rub the bread with a cut clove of garlic; drizzle with some good extra virgin olive oil, sprinkle some salt and pepper on the bread. Wash the tomatoes, squeeze them to remove the seeds and cut them in chunks. Place in a bowl, add the chopped basil, some sea salt and pepper, sprinkle with extra-virgin olive oil and a little vinegar. Spread on bread.

Bruschetta has recently become very popular in the UK and has now many versions. In Italy, especially in the Campania region, thanks to its large production of tomatoes, it has been around for centuries. It originates as a snack for farmers. The tomato was spread on a thick, rough slice of home-made bread and the bruschetta was eaten during their breaks. The name probably comes from the rough brush that was used to clean the horses and farm animals which was called "Brusca".

Courgette and leek quiche
Ingredients and method

1 pack puff or short crust pastry (if you decide to make your own pastry follow the easy recipe as given on the BBC website)

2 courgette

2 leeks

½ tub single cream

2 eggs

100g cheddar cheese, grated

30g Parmesan cheese, grated

½ tsp. cinnamon

3 tbsp. extra-virgin olive oil

Salt and pepper

Preheat the oven to 190°

Lightly butter an oven proof dish (20-25cm round); line the dish with the pastry (bought or homemade) and leave some pastry to go over the edge; in a frying pan, fry the leek (washed and cut into small pieces) for 5 minutes; add the courgette (washed and diced) and let cook for another 10 minutes, season with salt. Break the eggs in a jug and whisk; add the cream, the cheeses, the cinnamon, the salt and pepper and whisk. When the leek and courgette have cooled down, place them on the pastry and pour the egg mixture on them. Cook for about 25-30 minutes or until the mixture has risen.

Stuffed mushrooms and tomatoes
Ingredients and method

4 large chestnut mushrooms

100g cheddar cheese

50g breadcrumbs

1tbsp. chopped parsley

1tbsp. chopped basil

1 clove garlic, chopped

2 tbsp. extra-virgin olive oil

Parmesan cheese

Salt and pepper

Wash the mushrooms and dry them; remove stems and scoop as much as you can of the inside, without breaking the caps. Put the parsley, garlic, basil, cheddar cheese, stems and whatever you were able to scoop and the breadcrumbs in a blender; add some salt and pepper and some olive oil and blend until a thick mixture has formed. Remove from blender, add 2 tbsp. of single cream, mix well and then scoop mixture into mushroom caps; sprinkle with Parmesan cheese. Place on a greased oven dish and bake in a pre-heated oven (200°) for about 20 minutes (cover the dish with foil for the first 10 minutes).

The same procedure/ingredients can be used for stuffed tomatoes (wash the tomatoes, scoop the inside, try to remove as many seeds as you can, and place face down to dry before filling).

Fruit salad in lemon juice
Ingredients and method

2 peaches

2 apricots

2 pears

1 mango

Wash and peel the fruit; cut it into small cubes. Place in a bowl; dissolve 2 tsp. of sugar with the juices of 1 lemon and 1 orange and pour over fruit. Let it cool in fridge before serving. Serve with vanilla ice cream.

I thought I had been quite successful so far in my first few days as the Cardinal's chef but I needed to keep it up and think of new and interesting dishes that could be delicious and nutritious at the same time. Who knows, in a few months I might even be given a mark 10!

Miscellany

Other Italian regions use nuts in their traditional recipes for food and drinks; one that comes immediately to mind, associated with the clergy, is the famous Frangelico; this is a brand of noisette (hazelnut) and herb-flavoured liqueur (coloured with caramel) which is produced in Canale, Piedmont. The distinctive *Frangelico* bottle is designed to look like a friar in his brown habit with a white knotted rope tied around its waist. Apparently, the name of the liqueur comes from a legend of a hermit, Fra Angelico, who was the creator of herbal liqueurs. However, the bottle itself looks more like the habit of a Franciscan friar, while the liqueur's likely namesake, the famous painter Fra Angelico (d.1455), was a Dominican, whose robe was white and had no belt.

So many Italian regions use almonds in their cuisine. Sicilian sweets and pastries all contain almonds mixed with ricotta cheese and the combination is delicious. The famous almond nougat's best recipe comes from Sicily and the best marzipan sweets also come from there.

Ricotta is a very versatile cheese that can be used to make delicious pasta sauces as well as very tasty cakes. Ricotta can also be used for all types of cheese cakes. As ricotta is 100% fat free, it is a favourite for those on a diet.

Almost all Sicilian sweets and cakes are flavoured with almonds and make with ricotta cheese. The N'zuddi, for instance, are biscuits cooked with orange and almonds and made in the shape of a square as a tribute to the Patron Saint of Messina, Madonna della Lettera, to commemorate the time when a delegation from the town, that had just been converted to Christianity by St Paul, wishing to know the Virgin Mary, went to Jerusalem and came back in 43AD with a letter from Mary rolled and tied with a strand of her hair. The name "N'Zuddi" appears to be an abbreviation of the name Vincenzo in Sicilian dialect that would be "Vincinzuddu", as these biscuits were originally made by some Vincentians Nuns near Mount Etna.

For your eyes only!

Penne with ricotta and tomato sauce - sole fillets in orange sauce - carrot cake

Penne with ricotta and tomato sauce
Ingredients and method

200g Penne

100g ricotta cheese

2 tbsp. extra-virgin olive oil

2 cloves garlic

5/6 leaves fresh basil

1 x 400g tin of good quality chopped tomatoes

Salt

Freshly ground pepper

Parmesan cheese

Pour the oil in a large non-stick pan, add the garlic and when this changes colour, add the tomatoes. Let simmer for 30 minutes, add the basil, salt and pepper to taste and let cook for another 5 minutes. Remove from heat and leave to cool.

Bring water to the boil in a large pan, season with salt and put the penne in. Cook for about 10-12 minutes until cooked "al dente". While the pasta is cooking add the ricotta to the tomato sauce and stir well until you obtain a homogeneous cream. Drain the pasta, pour into the sauce, mix well and sprinkle with Parmesan cheese and pepper.

Sole fillets in orange sauce
Ingredients and method

2 sole fillets (with skin)

3 tbsp. plain flour

2 tbsp. extra-virgin olive oil and 1tbsp.butter

Juice of 1 orange

Salt and pepper

Check that all the bones have been removed from the fish. On a plate season the flour with salt and pepper and coat the fish well in it. Heat the oil and butter in a non-stick pan, add the fish, skin side down for about 2 minutes. Using a large spatula turn the fish and cook for another minute before adding the juice of 1 orange. Cook for another minute, remove from the heat and serve immediately.

Carrot cake
Ingredients and method

For the cake

> 2 tsp. cinnamon
> 2 large carrots, grated
> 150g self-raising flour
> 200g caster sugar
> 200ml vegetable oil
> 2 eggs
> 60g chopped walnuts (optional)

For the icing

> 150g cream cheese
> 60g butter (softened)
> 250g icing sugar
> 60g chopped walnuts

Stir together the eggs and the sugar in a large bowl, mix well. In another bowl stir together the flour, the oil and the cinnamon, add to the eggs and sugar, mix until well blended; add the carrot (and walnuts). Divide the cake mixture into two greased round cake tins (approx. 20 cm). Bake in a pre-heated oven for 25 minutes or until a toothpick inserted into the cake comes out clean. Remove from the oven and leave to cool.

In a bowl mix together the cream cheese, the butter, add the sugar and stir well; add the walnuts and use the mixture to fill in between the two layers and on top of the cake.

It is difficult to ascertain where the modern carrot cake came from. It seems that it was eaten in medieval times as a carrot pudding and gradually developed into the modern carrot cake. Apparently, carrots were used in the Middle Ages instead of sugar as sweeteners, as these were hard and costly to obtain.

It is a very well-known fact that all orange/red coloured vegetables and fruit are very good for your eyesight!

Time to relax

At this point I was able to relax: I think my cooking had been accepted and I had become more confident in my "experiments".

Sometimes I would have gladly offered champagne with some of my desserts but my finances did not allow such a luxury. Instead, one evening I offered the following. *Risotto allo champagne (champagne risotto - which can also be made with Prosecco) - prawns on skewers served on a bed of courgette and carrot - stuffed peaches*

Risotto allo champagne
Ingredients and method

200g Italian Arborio rice.

300ml vegetable stock (1 cube)

50g Parmesan cheese

2 tbsp. extra-virgin olive oil

20g unsalted butter

1 small spring onion

½ tub single cream

½ glass of champagne or prosecco

Chop the spring onion and place it in a large pan with the olive oil, fry for 5 minutes until the onion is soft. Add the rice and stir until it is well coated. Add the stock a little at the time and cook gently; when the rice is almost cooked, add the champagne, continue stirring to avoid sticking, if needed, add more stock until the rice is cooked. Season with a little salt according to taste. Fold in a little cream and stir one last time. Remove from the heat, finish your risotto by adding a knob of butter (so that the rice is nice and creamy), add the Parmesan cheese and serve immediately.

You may know that champagne was invented by Dom Pérignon. Dom Pérignon (1638–1715) was a Benedictine monk and cellar master at the Benedictine abbey in Hautvillers. He was a pioneer in a number of winemaking techniques.

Prawns on skewers served on a bed of courgette and carrot
Ingredients and method

2 courgette

2 carrots

1 tsp. chopped onion

4 tbsp. extra-virgin olive oil

1 tbsp. lemon juice

½ tbsp. balsamic vinegar

1 clove garlic, finely chopped

1 tbsp. soya sauce

500g raw king prawns, peeled

Cut the courgette and carrots lengthways and make thin batons out of them. Heat 2 tbsp. oil in a large pan, add the onion and fry for 2/3 minutes; add the carrots and courgette, cover and cook on a gentle heat for about 10/15 minutes. Remove the lid and cook for another 5 minutes. Put to one side. Place the garlic, oil, soya sauce, lemon juice, the vinegar, salt and pepper in a bowl and whisk until all the ingredients are nicely combined. Add the prawns and coat them evenly. Cover and leave them to soak for 30 minutes. Heat the oven grill, remove the prawns from the sauce and thread into metal skewers. Grill on each side for about 2/3 minutes until the prawns are fully cooked. Heat the vegetables, place them in a large dish, put the prawns on top of the vegetables and serve immediately.

Stuffed peaches
Ingredients and method

2 large nectarines or yellow peaches

3-4 amaretti biscuits

1 tsp. sugar

1 tbsp. walnut, chopped

3 tbsp. crème fraîche

Preheat the oven to 180°. Cut the peaches in half and remove the stone. Scoop out some of the flesh making sure not to break the skin. Crush the amaretti using a rolling pin and stir them in a bowl with the peach flesh, the walnut, the sugar and the crème fraîche. Grease an oven-proof dish, place the peaches cut side up on the tray and spoon the mixture into them. Bake for 10/15 minutes. You can serve with cream on the side.

Peaches and nectarines originated from China. They have been cultivated there for 5,000 years! From there the cultivation spread to Syria, Persia (from where the name of the tree Prunus Persica Vulgaris comes from) and Greece where it was already known in the 4thc BC. In Italy the cultivation started in the 1st c BC; it was brought to America by the Spanish "Conquistadores".

Beware: melon on the menu!

Other Italian regions offer different specialties and the use of vegetables is very common when cooking pasta. Some southern regions, like Apulia, Calabria and Campania, all have pasta dishes prepared with some typical vegetable. *Parma ham and melon - Orecchiette con cime di rapa - from Apulia (ear shaped pasta with turnip tops) - tiramisu'*

Parma ham with melon
Ingredients and method

> 100g Parma ham
>
> 1 ripe melon

Cut the melon in half, remove the seeds and the fibres from the centre. Obtain 5 or 6 slices from each half and remove the skin. Place 2 or 3 slices of melon on each plate and put 2 or 3 slices of Parma ham on the melon. Sometimes the simplest recipes are also the tastiest.

Pope Paul II (1417-1471) was a Pope famous for ...his chef. Bartolomeo Platina wrote and published a cookbook, the first ever cookbook printed on a press, in 1470. Among the advice he gave about the consequences of eating certain food stuffs, he warned about eating melon on a full stomach, encouraging people to have melon as a starter or appetizer. This would prove to be a sad prediction as Pope Paul II died after eating two big melons! But, in keeping with tradition, he might have been poisoned!

Orecchiette con cime di rapa
Ingredients and method

200g orecchiette (these are available at Italian delicatessen shops and in some supermarkets but if you can't find this shape, buy a shell shape)

400g young cime di rapa (turnip tops) or purple sprouting broccoli

1 clove garlic thinly sliced

3 tbsp. extra-virgin olive oil

3 tbsp. breadcrumbs

3 tbsp. grated Parmesan cheese or pecorino cheese

Cut the leaves and stalks into 5-10cm lengths and keep the tender florets intact. Discard the hard main stem. Bring the water for the pasta to the boil in a large pan, add 2 tbsp. salt. When the water boils put the pasta and the cime di rape into the pan and cook for approximately 12 minute. While the pasta is cooking heat the oil in a frying pan, add the garlic and fry for about 2-3 minutes, add the breadcrumbs, remove the pan from the heat and remove the garlic. When the pasta is cooked, add a few tablespoons of the pasta water to the frying pan, drain the pasta well and toss it into the frying pan, sauté briefly, season with salt and pepper (if needed). Serve with grated Parmesan or Pecorino cheese.

You could also add to the frying pan some anchovies fillets and stir until dissolved.

Tiramisu'
Ingredients and method

150g mascarpone cheese

300g double cream

50ml Marsala wine or similar

3 tbsp. caster sugar

200ml strong coffee

100g sponge fingers (savoiardi)

20g dark chocolate

1 tsp cocoa powder

Put the mascarpone, the cream, the Marsala and the sugar in a bowl. Whisk until all the ingredients are well combined and have reached the consistency of whipped cream. Have a nice serving dish ready. In another dish pour the coffee and dip in the savoiardi turning them until they are soaked (they should not be soggy). Start a layer with half of the biscuits then spread over them half of the cream, grate over this most of the chocolate. Continue with a second layer until all the biscuits are used. Finish with cream on top. Cover and put in the fridge for a couple of hours before serving. Before serving dust with the cocoa powder and grate the rest of the chocolate on top.

It is not known where Tiramisu' (literally pick-me-up) originates from. Some date it to 1960 claiming it was made by a famous chef in a restaurant in Treviso, Veneto Region. Some state it came from Lomdardy. There are even claims that the first Tiramisu' was invented by a chef from Siena on the occasion of the visit to the city by Cosimo III de' Medici, Gran Duke of Tuscany (1600).

Grandma's recipes

Polenta pasticciata (cornmeal mush) with stracchino
and Parmesan cheese - fennel, walnut and chicory salad
- apple cake. (my grandma could make this blind folded)

As polenta is very filling, it needs to be followed by something
quite light.

Polenta pasticciata
Ingredients and method

100g coarse cornmeal

100ml milk

350ml water

½ tsp. salt

30g butter

100g stracchino cheese (or light brie if you cannot find stracchino)

100g mozzarella cheese

30g Parmesan cheese

To make a proper polenta requires patience and time (cooked polenta is already available in supermarkets but I believe the end result is less tasty when using ready made polenta).

In a large pan bring the milk and the water to the boil, add the salt. Add the cornmeal in thin streams whisking non-stop. Stir for a few minutes until the cornmeal thickens. Turn the heat down and stir every 3-4 minutes to prevent from getting stuck to the pan. Cook for 30 minutes. Remove from the heat and add the butter. Grease an oven dish with butter. Put a layer of polenta on the dish, put the stracchino (or brie if you cannot find stracchino) and the mozzarella cut in small chunks covering the whole surface; add another layer of polenta and carry on like this until all the polenta and cheese have been used. Sprinkle with Parmesan cheese and a few blobs of butter. Cook on a pre-heated oven (180°) for about 20 minutes until the polenta gets a nice golden colour. Wear an oven glove when stirring as polenta tends to "bubble' and can burn you.

Pope John XXIII (1881-1963), who was responsible for calling the Second Vatican Council, was known as a charismatic leader but also for being a good eater. He was born into a large family in the Bergamo province, Lombardy region, close to the Alps. He loved polenta which was sent regularly to Rome from the Bergamo countryside and prepared by the Sisters looking after his kitchen. The cornmeal would turn into a delicious, steaming meal which would take him back to his "peasant origins".

Fennel, walnut and chicory salad
Ingredients and method

1 fennel

30g walnuts

1 chicory salad

Salt, pepper, extra-virgin olive oil, balsamic vinegar

Thinly cut the fennel and the chicory; put them in a salad bowl and add the walnuts. Season with salt, pepper, extra-virgin olive oil and balsamic vinegar.

Apple cake
Ingredients and method

200g self-raising white flour

2 granny smith apples, skinned and cut in thin pieces

2 egg yolk

1 egg white

100g sugar

100g butter, melted

1 tsp cinnamon

Mix the sugar and the 2 egg yolks together. Wisk the egg white until fluffy; in a large bowl add the butter to the flour and a little at a time add the egg white to it. Add the cut apples, the cinnamon, the sugar and egg mixture and a little milk. Mix well until all the ingredients are well amalgamated and you have a soft mixture. Butter an oven dish, pour the mixture in and put in a preheated oven (180˚) and cook for 40 minutes or until a golden colour has formed. When the cake has cooled down, sprinkle a little icing sugar on it.

Winter warmers

Pasta ai quattro formaggi (four cheeses pasta) - *"carne alla pizzaiola" (meat with tomato sauce "pizza-style")* - *vanilla cheesecake* I offered the above one winter evening and, although cheese might not be very healthy if you have high cholesterol, when eaten in moderation it is not harmful!

Pasta ai quattro formaggi
Ingredients and method

200g penne

50g stracchino

50g gorgonzola

50g gruyere

30g Parmesan cheese

30g butter

Bring the water to the boil in a large pan. Add some salt and the penne. Mix well. Turn the heat down. While the pasta is cooking, put the cheese (not the Parmesan) in a bowl and melt it over the pasta boiling water. When the pasta is cooked pour it over the melted cheese, add the butter and the Parmesan cheese and stir well and serve immediately.

Did you know that Pope Pius II (1405-1464) had a real passion for cheese? It seems that he loved cacio cheese made with ewe's milk. He was born in a village which he had restored after becoming Pope and made into a perfect Renaissance town and was known for walking on the hills and trying out the local milk. He of course declared that the milk produced in Corsignano (his model village now called Pienza, a little jewel town, near Siena), was the best in Italy and the cheese produced with it was absolutely the best.

Carne alla pizzaiola
Ingredients and method

4 slices frying steaks (thinly cut)
200g can of chopped tomatoes
1 clove of garlic
a handful of parsley
a handful of oregano
20g extra-virgin olive oil
Salt, pepper

Chop the garlic and the parsley. Heat the meat in the oil, put the chopped garlic and parsley and the oregano on top of the meat; add the chopped tomatoes and a little water, season with salt and pepper. Cover the pan and cook for about ten minutes.

It seems that this dish originates from the Neapolitan cuisine and as the pizza and the pizzaiola share three main ingredients, tomato, garlic and oregano, the dish was given this name.

Vanilla cheesecake
Ingredients and method

2 tbsp. vanilla extract

100g crème fraîche

100g mascarpone cheese

1 packet digestive biscuits (300g) – crumbled

100g unsalted butter

150g icing sugar

Melt the butter in the microwave or in a pan on a low heat; mix the butter with the biscuits so that they are all well coated. Press them evenly in a greased oven-proof tin and put in the fridge for at least 30 minutes.

Mix the mascarpone with the icing sugar and the vanilla extract, beat in the crème fraîche until you have a thick creamy mixture. Remove the base from the fridge, pour the cream on it and level with a knife. Put in the fridge for a couple of hours before serving.

Vanilla derived from orchids native of Mexico. It has an amazing history filled with intrigue and piracy. It is the invisible component of many medicines to make them taste better and of food stuff and drinks. It was the Spaniards, after they conquered the Aztecs, who brought the vanilla beans to Spain and for many years vanilla combined with cacao was only enjoyed by the nobility and the very rich. When Queen Elizabeth I's personal apothecary (the modern pharmacist), Hugh Morgan (1530-1613), recommended that vanilla should be used by itself, its full flavour was revealed and really appreciated. Nowadays Vanilla is cultivated all over the world, from Madagascar to Indonesia, from the Caribbean and the Seychelles to India.

By now, a very confident cook!

Cannelloni with spinach and ricotta cheese - vitello tonnato - apple crumble with custard

Cannelloni with spinach and ricotta cheese
Ingredients and method

To make the white sauce: 50g of butter, 50g of plain flour, about 500ml of whole milk. Melt the butter in a saucepan on a low heat. When the butter is melted add the flour and stir continuously to avoid sticking and until a paste is formed. Add the milk little by little while stirring again continuously. Finish adding the milk until you get a smooth sauce, cook for a few minutes until the sauce has thickened.

To make the tomato sauce: thinly slice a small onion and fry it with 1 clove of garlic in a pan with some olive oil. When the onion and garlic are golden, add two cans of chopped tomato, some basil leaves and 200ml of water. Simmer very gently until the sauce has reduced and it is very thick.

To make the cannelloni: You can either buy dried cannelloni tubes at most supermarkets or, which is a much better alternative, use part-boiled lasagne sheets and roll them into tubes. Of course you can make your own pasta but it will take you ages!

Before rolling the lasagne into tubes, prepare the filling: sauté a large bag of spinach with some garlic in a large saucepan (buy the ready to cook already washed spinach as it is less watery); cook it until tender and all the residual water has evaporated. In a bowl mix two tubs of ricotta cheese with one egg and a little amount of grated nutmeg. Mix together. When the spinach is cold add to the ricotta and mix well.

Cook the lasagne sheets (two for each guest or more depending on the appetite) for about 5-6 minutes. Add oil to the boiling water to avoid sticking and when they are cooked put them in a bowl of cold water (again to prevent them from sticking). You have to be quick at this now: on each sheet put a tablespoon (or even a little more) of the filling, roll it into a sort of sausage shape along the long edge, close it and brush it with some milk. Place the cannelloni into a greased oven pan open side down. Repeat process until all sheets have been used.

Cover the cannelloni with the white sauce and the tomato sauce; sprinkle some Parmesan cheese on top. Cook in a pre-heated oven at 180°/190° until brown for 30/40 minutes (do not let the cannelloni burn – hint: cover them with foil for 20 minutes and then uncover for the rest of the cooking time).

Vitello tonnato
Ingredients and method

300g turkey breast fillet (this recipe should be made with veal meat but I use turkey instead and tonnato means with a tuna flavour)

1 stalk celery

1 carrot

3 bay leaves

1 clove garlic

2 tbsp. extra-virgin olive oil

½ glass white wine

Water

2 tsp. capers

1 tin tuna in olive oil, drained (50/75 g will be enough)

1½ boiled eggs

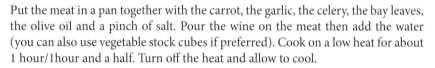

Put the meat in a pan together with the carrot, the garlic, the celery, the bay leaves, the olive oil and a pinch of salt. Pour the wine on the meat then add the water (you can also use vegetable stock cubes if preferred). Cook on a low heat for about 1 hour/1hour and a half. Turn off the heat and allow to cool.

While the meat is cooling prepare the sauce. Put the tuna, the boiled eggs and the capers in the blender, add a little olive oil and a little of the cooking water until the sauce gets to a creamy texture.

When the meat is cold, cut it into thin slices and place on a serving dish. Add a little balsamic vinegar to the sauce and spread it onto the meat; garnish with a few capers.

Apple crumble with custard
Ingredients and method

For the crumble

  150g plain flour

  100g brown sugar (unrefined)

  100g unsalted butter

For the filling

  2 granny smith apples (I like the sour taste of Granny Smith but you can use cooking apples)

  25g brown sugar (unrefined)

  1 tbsp. plain flour)

  1 tsp. cinnamon

  ½ glass milk

Put the flour and sugar in a bowl and mix well. Rub the butter (cut into small pieces) into the flour mixture and work it with your hands until it looks like breadcrumbs.

Place the apples in a pan with the sugar, flour and cinnamon. Add the milk and cook gently for a few minutes making sure not to break the fruit. Let it cool.

Butter a 18 cm ovenproof dish. Distribute the fruit on the whole surface, sprinkle the crumble mixture on top of the fruit. Bake in a pre-heated oven 180°) for about 30/35 minutes or until you can see bubbles on the surface. Serve on its own or with cream/custard.

It is said that Pope John Paul II's (1920-2005) favourite food was a cake that he used to eat in his hometown of Wadowice when he was a young boy. It was made with two layers of puff pastry stuffed with whipped cream, buttercream and custard. The cake was originally called "kremowka" but was renamed "kremowka papieska" (papal cream cake) after John Paul II visited the town in 1999 and recollected the time when as a young boy and as a student he used to eat them. Once, after passing his high school exams and in a contest with friends, he is said to have managed to eat 18!

The last supper

Lasagne al pesto (pesto lasagna) - Orata alla mediterranea (Mediterranean gilthead bream) - creamy apricots

Lasagne al pesto
Ingredients and method

250g egg lasagne (most supermarkets sell ready-made lasagne sheets)

Pesto sauce (please see recipe on pages 26)

White sauce (please see recipe on page 47)

100g cheddar

50g gorgonzola cheese (optional)

50g parmesan cheese

Bring some water to the boil in a large pan. Add a little vegetable oil to the boiling water and some salt and put the lasagne sheets in, two at a time. Boil for about 5 minutes and place on a bowl with cold water. Drain. Proceed like this until you finish the sheets. Cut the cheddar and the gorgonzola into small pieces. In a bowl mix the white sauce (once cooled) and the pesto so to obtain a creamy sauce, add a little milk if needed. Sprinkle the creamy sauce on the bottom of a buttered oven-dish and make layers of lasagne, cheese, sauce, Parmesan cheese and so on until you finish all the ingredients. Make sure to finish with plenty of sauce and with a sprinkle of Parmesan cheese. Bake on a preheated oven (180°) for 20/25 minutes or until browned.

As I said earlier on in the book, pesto is an excellent sauce for gnocchi. I prepared "gnocchi al pesto" for the Cardinal a few times and he used to ask me: "why gnocchi, is it Thursday today"? He remembered that during his time in Rome, it was customary to eat gnocchi on Thursdays, fish on Friday and trippa (tripe) on Saturday!

Orata alla mediterranea
Ingredients and method

1lb fresh sea bream (whole)

3 tbsp. extra-virgin olive oil

1 clove garlic

Rosemary (a couple of stems)

Sea salt and fresh grounded pepper

1 tsp. fennel seeds

Wash the fish and dry it. Make a cut in the backbone. Make a marinade with the oil, the salt and pepper, the garlic, the chopped rosemary and the fennels seeds. Brush the fish with the marinade making sure that some goes into the cut. Leave the fish to soak the mixture for about ½ hour. Place the fish on a greased baking dish making sure that you spoon all the marinade on the fish. Put some rosemary stems on top of the fish. Cook in a pre-heated oven 180°/200° for 15 minutes. Serve with some wedges of lemon.

Creamy apricots
Ingredients and method

4 apricots cut in half and stoned

2 tbsp. Porto or good red wine wine

50 ml crème fraîche

50g walnuts, chopped

1 tbsp. icing sugar

Put the apricots, the porto and a little water in a pan, bring to the boil and let bubble for about 2 minutes. Remove from the heat and leave to cool. Mix the crème fraîche, the sugar and the walnuts together; spoon over the cooled apricots and put in fridge until ready to serve.

Normally the Cardinal and the Monsignor would choose the wine themselves, but on this occasion I provided it. I have to say this is a very good wine and should be appreciated in little sips and in moderate quantities. The name of this wine is Châteauneuf – du – Pape made around the village of that name in the Rhône wine region in southeastern France. Although much is known about it, not many people know that this wine is strongly associated with papal history. When the Archbishop of Bordeaux became Pope as Clement V (1264-1314) in 1308, he moved the papacy to the city of Avignon and during the twentyseven year duration of his and Pope John XXII (1249-1334) papacies, they did much to promote this wine and all the wines from the Burgundy region. During John XXII papacy, the wines of this area became known as "Vin du Pape". "Vin du Pape" later became Châteauneuf du Pape as John XXII was also responsible for the construction of the castle which is the symbol of the appellation (AOC – Appelation d'Origine Contrôlée)

Final vote!

This was the last entry in my little collection of recipes which were prepared in the Cardinal's kitchen and, although I still occasionally cook for him, one thing I am proud of is that, finally, on this particular evening, I was given a mark 10 for taste and presentation!

It has been a real pleasure and a privilege to become, even for a short time, the "Cardinal Chef".

Some additional recipes you may wish to try

Trofie al pesto with potatoes and green beans
(you may be able to find this type of pasta in some supermarkets or in Italian delicatessen; if not, look for trenette or bavette)

Ingredients and method

Ingredients and method:

200g Trofie, trenette or bavette pasta

100g green beans

125g potatoes

2 tbsp extra-virgin olive oil

pesto sauce ingredients and method, please see recipe on page 26.

Bring the water for the pasta to the boil in a large pan. Add the peeled and washed potatoes cut into cubes and the washed green beans cut in half (after you have snapped the tips and removed the filaments). Add the pasta and salt to taste. Cook the pasta "al dente", place the pesto in a large bowl, add a little cooking water, drain the pasta and pour it into the bowl. Stir well and serve immediately.

Oven baked red radicchio and walnuts
Ingredients and method

2 large heads red radicchio (round or oblong – the oblong version can be more bitter that the round)

30g walnuts, chopped

2 tbsp extra-virgin olive oil

2 tbsp single cream

20g Parmesan cheese

Wash the radicchio thoroughly and dry it on kitchen towel. Cut it in quarters (lengthwise). Butter an oven pan and place the radicchio on it; sprinkle the walnuts on the radicchio, pour the cream on it and lastly add the Parmisan cheese. Cover with foil, bake in a preheated oven (180°) for about 15 minutes, remove the foil and bake for a further 5 minutes.

Red radicchio is a very versatile type of chicory and can be used to make delicious sauces for pasta or to prepare a very tasty risotto as well as being used to make wonderful salads. It is bitter and spicy in taste and it is naturally rich in intybin, a sedative and analgesic. Pliny the Elder (23-79 AD), the famous naturalist/author/philosopher and an army commander of the Roman Empire and personal friend of the Emperor Vespasian, believed that radicchio was a good blood purifier and helped with insomnia. Radicchio was first cultivated in the fifteenth century in the Veneto and Trentino regions of Italy and it is now produced in many other Italian regions and European countries.

Oven baked fennel and pine nuts
Ingredients and method

2 large fennels

20g pine nuts, roughly chopped

2 tbsp extra-virgin olive oil

2 tbsp. single cream

20g Parmesan cheese (grated)

salt to taste

Pre-heat oven to 180°. Wash the fennels and remove the outside layer. Cut the fennels in 4 or 5 slices of 1cm. Put the fennel pieces on an oiled oven dish. Sprinkle the pine nuts on them, the cream, some salt and the oil. Finish by sprinkling the Parmesan cheese on top. Put them in the oven and bake for 15 minutes or until the fennels have browned.

Pliny the Elder (him again) believed strongly in the power of fennel. In his "Naturalis Historie" he lists more than 20 different afflictions that can be treated by fennel. King Edward I of England (1239-1307) used fennel seeds not only for seasoning food but also as a digestive and appetite inhibitor. Fennel seeds were used by the faithful on those Fast Days imposed by the Church when they needed to go through the day without feeling hungry. It is believed that in Mediaeval times fennel was hung over doors to safeguard the inhabitants from malicious phenomenon. Many other physicians and naturalists from ancient Greece to the Romans, from Mediaeval times to today's herbalists, swear by the fennel's medicinal therapeutic properties.

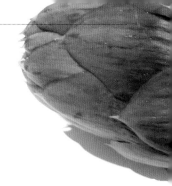

Fried artichokes
Ingredients and method

2 large artichokes

1 egg

2 tbsp. flour

2 tbsp. milk

Vegetable oil

Start by removing the tough outer leaves of the artichokes. Cut the tops and the stem just below the base. Cut each artichoke in eight parts and eliminate the annoying fluffy stuff inside them. Put them in water and lemon juice to prevent from blackening. Beat the egg in a bowl with the flour and the milk. Add some salt. Pour the cut artichokes in the batter and let them soak for a few minutes turning them once or twice so that the whole surface is covered. Heat some vegetable (sesame or sunflower) oil in a non-stick pan and when hot dip the artichoke pieces one by one paying attention that they do not stick together. Turn them in order to fry them on both sides. Fry them for about 2/3 minutes on each side, remove them from the oil, drain them on kitchen towel. Sprinkle some chopped parsley on top (optional) and serve hot. You may wish to add a little French mustard to the batter. You may also wish to squeeze a little lemon juice on them (again, optional).

According to legend, the first artichoke had been a "mortal girl" called Cynara until..... she met Zeus. When Zeus saw her he fell in love and took her to live on Olympia. But she grew homesick and one day she went to visit her mortal parents without telling him. Zeus discovered her conduct and became so angry that he sent her back to earth and transformed her into a plant: the artichoke! The artichoke is renowned for its digestive properties. A very popular Italian bitter liqueur is made with artichokes and 12 other herbs. It is called Cynar! It is drunk after a large meal as a digestif.

Tagliatelle alla Papalina (skullcap)
Ingredients and method

150/200g fettuccine (or tagliatelle)

30g chopped onions

50g cured ham (cut into strips)

100g single cream

1 egg

1 egg yolk

30g unsalted butter

30g Parmesan cheese

pepper and salt to taste

Heat the butter and the onions on a low heat and cook for about 5 minutes adding 4 tbsp. of water. Add the ham stirring all the time and cook for another minute. Turn off and put aside. Bring the water for the pasta to the boil, add some salt and cook the fettuccine "al dente". While the pasta is cooking break the eggs into a bowl, add the cream and stir with a whisk. Add the Parmesan cheese and salt and pepper to taste. When the pasta is ready pour it into the ham sauce, add the egg mixture and mix well for a few moments until all the ingredients are nicely blended together. Serve hot.

It is said that this tasty dish was created for Cardinal Eugenio Pacelli, the future Pope Pius XII (1876-1958), by the chef of the restaurant providing meals to the Vatican. Apparently the Cardinal asked for a new dish while at the same time respecting the traditional Roman cuisine. This is what the chef came up with which is a variant of the "pasta alla carbonara".

Aubergine and melted cheese
(this is a very quick and tasty dish when you only have a little time to prepare a delicious starter).

Ingredients and method

1 large or two medium aubergines

100g smoked cheese (cheddar or similar)

2 tbsp. extra-virgin olive oil

salt

Wash and cut the aubergines into 1cm round slices. Dip the slices in the oil seasoned with salt. Pre-heat the oven to 180°. Butter an oven dish and place the oiled aubergine slices onto the dish and bake for 10 minutes or so turning once. Cut the cheese into 50mm pieces. Place the cheese over the aubergines trying to cover with the cheese the whole surface. Bake for a further 10 minutes or until the cheese has melted. Serve immediately.

Gnocchi alla romana (semolina gnocchi)
Ingredients and method

125g semolina

500ml milk

50g butter

1 egg yolk

60g parmesan cheese

Salt – nutmeg (grated)

Bring the milk to a boil, add some salt and the nutmeg; pour in the semolina whisking all the time to prevent lumps from forming. Cook for ten minutes or so (wear some kitchen gloves as the semolina can burn your skin when it thickens as it tends to squirt out of the pan. Remove from the heat and put the butter into the mixture and ¾ of the Parmesan cheese, stir well. Pour the semolina onto an oiled surface and, with wet hands, level the mixture to a layer of about 1 cm. When the semolina has cooled down, cut as many discs as you can, with the help of a small round glass. Butter an oven-dish, place the discs in the pan partly going over the edge of each disc. Once all the discs are in the dish, sprinkle them with melted butter and the Parmesan cheese. Bake in a pre-heated oven at 180° for about 20 minutes or until golden.

In Roman times, gnocchi were not made using potatoes but a semolina-porridge like mixture mixed with eggs. They are still found in the same shape all over Italy today, but in particular in Rome, they are oven-baked and are called "gnocchi alla romana".

Crêpes filled with pumpkin and cheese
Ingredients and method

For the crêpes (please see recipe and ingredients on page 17)

For the white sauce (please see recipe and ingredients on page 47)

½ of a pumpkin (or butternut squash, skinned)

half medium size onion

fennel seeds (crushed)

salt

1 cup milk

Start by making the crêpes and the white sauce. Fry the chopped onion in a large pan and add the thinly cut pumpkin. Mix a little and then add the milk. Lower the heat and let cook until the pumpkin is cooked and reduced to the consistency of a mash. Add the crushed fennel seeds and stir so that they are thoroughly blended. Let it cool. Place the crêpes on an oiled surface. Put a spoon of the pumpkin, some pieces of brie and a spoon of white sauce on them. Sprinkle with parmesan cheese and roll them firmly. Put the crêpes on a buttered oven dish, opening down. Put some more white sauce on them and sprinkle again with Parmesan cheese. Bake in a pre-heated oven (180°) for about 20 minutes. Serve hot.

Please note that this pumpkin sauce is delicious also to make lasagne. Use the recipe for pesto lasagna on page 50 and, instead of using the pesto, use this pumpkin sauce. It is mouth-watering!

Pumpkins are rich in vitamins A and B, potassium and iron and are very low in fat. Pumpkins are very versatile and used to make delicious soups, risotto, salads and my recipe above. Pumpkin is particularly used in autumn as it is harvested in October. Pumpkins carved during the Halloween week are to be seen outside the doors or at the windows of most houses. But not many may know that the Christian Church introduced the Feast of All Saints at the time when it was trying to divert the interest of people from pagan festivals. It seems that the word Halloween is a contraction of All Hallows, as 1st November was originally the Feast of All Hallows and 31st October All Hallows eve.

Layered vegetables
Ingredients and method

2 large potatoes

2 large carrots

1 pack washed spinach

Besciamella (white sauce – see ingredients and method on page 47)

Parmesan cheese

Gruyere cheese

Boil and mash separately the potatoes and carrots, season with salt and pepper Cook the spinach in a pan with a whole clove of garlic. When the spinach is ready, remove the excess water and the garlic and chop finely. Cover with white sauce the bottom of an oven dish, start the layers with the potato mash, slice some gruyere cheese on top, cover with white sauce and sprinkle with Parmesan cheese; follow this first layer with a spinach layer and proceed as above; then continue with a carrot layer in the same way. Once all the ingredients have been used, cover with white sauce and sprinkle with Parmesan cheese. Cook in a pre-heated oven (180°) for about 20/25 minutes or until golden brown. It can be served with a simple tomato sauce (recipe on page 47).

If we talk about spinach, we immediately think of Popeye, the sailor man and fictional character of a cartoon famous for his muscles derived from his spinach eating habit. Although associated with a fictional character, there may be some truth in the powers of this green vegetable. It is rich in vitamins and minerals and provides us with strong antioxidant defence. It is considered to be among the world's healthiest vegetables. If boiled, it is recommended that it should be for just 1 minute so not to lose its nutrients.

It is believed that spinach originated in ancient Persia and then gradually made its way to Europe where it was introduced by the Moors in Spain. It was actually known in England as the "Spanish vegetable".

Catherine de Medici (1519-1589) loved spinach and when she left her hometown of Florence to marry the King of France, Henry II, she took her cooks with her. Her cooks knew how to cook spinach in the ways she liked. The dishes prepared on a bed of spinach, to this day are known as "a la Florentine".

A little note to end

The Patron Saints of chefs are many, I will name but a few: St Fortunatus (Bishop of Poitiers and distinguished poet of VII century and St Radegund (who founded a Monastery of which Bishop Fortunato became the Chaplain). St Radegund was an excellent cook and used to prepare some delicious dishes which were described with many details in some of St Fortunato's letters; St Lawrence (died 258 AD) is considered to be the Patron Saint of cooks; St Martha (died 84 AD also

St Lawrence (Public domain)

Patron Saint of cooks); St Hildegarde (1098-1179) was a mystic nun who wrote many recipes; St Honoré (died 600 – he was Bishop of Amiens), considered the Patron Saint of bakers and pastry chefs; the famous Saint-Honore French cake is named after him!

St Martha (Public domain)

Therefore, if you wish your guests to be absolutely delighted by your offerings and want everything to be flawless, invoke the blessing of one or more of these Saints for a perfect evening!

Please note that all the recipes are for two people (generous portions!).

Notes

Notes

Notes